Literacy and Language
Anthology

6

Janey Pursglove and **Charlotte Raby**

Series developed by **Ruth Miskin**

OXFORD

UNIVERSITY PRESS

OXFORD
UNIVERSITY PRESS

Great Clarendon Street, Oxford, OX2 6DP,
United Kingdom

Oxford University Press is a department of the
University of Oxford. It furthers the University's
objective of excellence in research, scholarship,
and education by publishing worldwide.
Oxford is a registered trade mark of Oxford University
Press in the UK and in certain other countries

British Library Cataloguing in Publication Data
Data available

ISBN: 978-0-19-849382-2

10 9 8

Paper used in the production of this book is a natural,
recyclable product made from wood grown in sustainable
forests. The manufacturing process conforms to the
environmental regulations of the country of origin.

Printed in China by Golden Cup

Acknowledgements

Cover illustration by Roberto Weigand

Illustrations by: A3 Drawing Factory; Trevor Dunton;
Cesar Gonzales; Paul Hampson; Martin Sanders; David Semple;
Tom Spurling; Victor Tavares; Lazlo Veres; Bee Willey

The publishers would like to thank the following for the
permission to reproduce photographs: **p34t**: Eric Isselée/
Shutterstock; **p34m**: Fivespots/Shutterstock; **p34b**: Maxim
Kulko/Shutterstock; **p35t**: OUP; **p35b**: Face to face Bildagentur
GmbH/Alamy; **p36**: Bigstock; **p37**: OUP; **p38**: Bigstock; **p39**:
OUP; **p66l**: GoGo Images Corporation/Alamy; **p66r**: Vibe
Images/Alamy; **p67**: Gabi Moisa/Shutterstock.

Background images:
Photodisc/OUP; Hanna Hrakovich/Shutterstock; K.Thorsen/
Shutterstock; Hywit Dimyadi/Shutterstock; Fedorov Oleksiy/
Shutterstock; mart/Shutterstock; artida/Shutterstock

The authors and publisher are grateful to the following for
permission to reproduce copyright material:

Roger McGough p18 'Rabbit in Mixer Survives' from *Roger
McGough: Selected Poems* (Penguin, 2006), copyright © Roger
McGough 2006, reprinted by permission of PFD (www.pfd.
co.uk) on behalf of Roger McGough. **Michael Morpurgo p68**
'I Believe in Unicorns' from *Singing for Mrs Pettigrew* copyright
© Michael Morpurgo 2006, (Walker Books, 2006), reprinted by
permission of David Higham Associates.

We have made every effort to trace and contact all copyright
holders before publication. If notified, the publisher will
rectify any errors or omissions at the earliest opportunity.

The authors of the Fiction texts in this Anthology (excepting
those listed above) are as follows: **Geraldine McCaughrean
p4** *Robin Hood and the Golden Arrow*, text copyright © Oxford
University Press 2013; **Susan Price p24** Brashem's Tortoise,
text copyright © Susan Price; Susan Price has asserted her
right under the Copyright, Designs and Patents Act 1988 to
be identified as author of this material; **Lou Kuenzler p40**
Gone Away!; **p54** *The Elephant in the Room*, text copyright © Lou
Kuenzler 2013; Lou Kuenzler has asserted her right under the
Copyright, Designs and Patents Act 1988 to be identified as
author of this material.

The authors of the Non-fiction texts (excepting those listed
above) in this Anthology are as follows: **Adrian Bradbury
p14** 'The Sherwood Bugle'; **p15** 'Good Day!'; **p16** 'TV
Interview'; **p20** 'Should Humans *Really* Rule the Earth?'; **p22**
'Animals Rule! ...*But Which One?*'; **p34** 'Exotic pets – The Facts
and Figures'; **p36** 'Are You Sure You Really Want One?'; **p38**
'Protection of Exotic Pets Society'; **p51** 'Alexander Selkirk
Biography'; **p52** 'Castaway'; **p66** 'Make Memory Lapses a Thing
To Forget!'; **p67** 'Memoraid'; **p77** 'How Does a Story Become
a Manga Graphic Novel?'; texts copyright © Oxford University
Press 2013

TEACHERS:
For inspirational support plus
free resources and eBooks
www.oxfordprimary.co.uk

PARENTS:
Help your child's learning
with essential tips, phonics
support and free eBooks
www.oxfordowl.co.uk

Contents

Robin Hood and the Golden Arrow

AN ENGLISH LEGEND

Geraldine McCaughrean

England was a country in despair. When the wind blew through its forests, the trees groaned and the leaves sighed. It was a country ruled by foreign invaders, and while the Normans fed richly off the fat of the land, the conquered Saxons made do with the crumbs that were left.

King Richard had left to do battle in the Holy Lands, and in his absence his brother, Prince John, proved to be a **barbaric** ruler. He appointed men like the Sheriff of Nottingham and Guy of Gisborne: robber barons who sat in their granite castles and plotted to grow rich. They taxed and fined and robbed their Saxon subjects to the edge of starvation. They turned out-of-doors anyone too poor to pay, anyone too proud to pay, anyone whose property they wanted to take for themselves.

Robin of Locksley, for instance, was cheated of his father's land by Gisborne. Where was the law to protect him? The King would have given him justice, but law and justice no longer existed in the England ruled by Prince John.

Unless they lived on in Robin Hood.

That same Robin of Locksley, to preserve his life, slipped away into the green forest and disappeared. Soon afterwards, a mysterious figure was glimpsed by travellers, dressed all in green, with green-feathered arrows in his quiver and green mosses streaking his cheeks. No one knew at first whether the "Man of Sherwood" truly existed or not. But then strange things began to happen.

Fat Norman merchants were robbed of their gold, and the next day thin Saxon children found gold beneath their pillows. Cruel tax collectors were "relieved" of all their takings. Then money would fly in at the windows of widows, and flour fall like snow on starving villages. The mysterious Robin Hood was robbing the rich to feed the poor, and though the Norman soldiers hunted him like the hind, they could never find him. He had made the greenwood his own stronghold.

One by one, men who had suffered under Norman rule headed for the forest to join Robin Hood and to wear the "suit of green".

They were outlaws to the Normans, but heroes to the Saxons. Their very existence burned like a green gleam in the imagination, a flame of hope.

———————

"A tournament? Will there be archery?" asked Robin casually, waxing his bowstring with a stub of candle.

"That's the main event!" said Friar Tuck, tucking into his meal. "First prize is a golden arrow, presented by Gisborne himself." The friar's words **emerged** speckled with breadcrumbs and flecks of fat. "Open to any archer in the land. The Prince himself is going to be there, so they say."

Tuck was the only man in Robin's band not to wear the suit of green. In his brown habit, he could come and go to town unnoticed, unquestioned and bring them news, messages from wives and sweethearts, gifts from well-wishers. He was able, too, to deliver Robin's little "presents" to the poor of Nottingham.

Today his news was of a grand archery contest to be held within the castle walls. The outlaws, sitting around their campfire, greeted the news quietly, remembering other such festive holidays spent with their families.

"We know, without going, who's the best archer in England, don't we?" said Alan-a-Dale loyally, and all the outlaws shouted in one voice, "*Robin Hood!*"

"It would be pleasant to prove it, even so," murmured Robin.

"You *wouldn't!* You never would!" Much the Miller was horrified. "Tell him, Little John! Tell him it's too dangerous!"

"'S'probably a trap," said Will Scarlett gloomily. "The Sheriff probably means to lure Robin inside the castle – thinks he won't be able to resist competing for a stupid golden arrow."

"Let's not disappoint him, then!" declared Robin, jumping to his feet.

There was a streak of recklessness in Robin which scared his Merrie Men.

It was hard enough to keep alive in the **inhospitable** greenwood, without a man wilfully creeping into the stronghold of his worst enemy. And for what? An arrow of shiny gold that would not even fly?

The sun glinted on the golden arrow. The cushion it lay on was of blood-red velvet.

The castle grounds were bright with striped pavilions and painted flagpoles. Armour caught the sun and dazzled the eye. Chargers cloaked in cloth-of-gold stamped their hooves. It was a holiday in Nottingham and, for once, the brown and ragged townspeople were also allowed inside the castle precincts.

Entrants for the archery contest stood in a huddle: Prince John's best archers, the Sheriff's best henchmen, professional marksmen and amateur huntsmen. There were a few Saxons, too – arrowsmiths and bow-makers, for the most part. Impatiently they queued up to shoot at the distant butts.

Suddenly there was a flurry of excitement, as a young man in a green tunic was seized by castle guards and wrestled to the ground. "We knew you couldn't stay away, Robin Hood! Got you at last!"

But it was not Robin Hood at all, just a boy wearing green. Gisborne ground his teeth. He found archery **tedious**, and now he was obliged to sit through a whole afternoon of it.

Some arrows went wide, some buried themselves in the grass, ripping off their feather fletches. The butts looked like porcupines by the time all the bowmen had let fly their arrows. Last of all, an old man, bent and bearded, shuffled to the firing line, carrying his arrows in a basket. He began, with shaking hands, to fit an arrow to his bowstring.

"Get away, old man. Clear off!" they told him. "This is a young man's sport. Go home."

"Open to all, it said," croaked the old man.

"He's holding up the competition! Get rid of him!"

"Oh, let him make a fool of himself. Takes less time than arguing."

The old man nodded and doddered, peered down the field at the butts as if he could barely see them, then feebly tugged back on his bowstring. The arrow plunged into the golden heart of the target.

"Fluke."

"Lucky!"

"Not half bad, Grandpa."

The competition continued, with everyone disqualified who did not hit gold. Round by round it became harder – the butts were moved further off – and more bowmen were **eliminated**. But the luck of the old man held. The crowd began to warm to him: he was a ragged Saxon, after all. Every time he fired, they cheered. Every time a Norman missed, they cheered, too.

It came down to just three men: a Norman sergeant-at-arms, hand-picked by Guy of Gisborne, a pretty French knight in chequered velvet…and the old man, frail and lame, whose clothes had more holes in them than the canvas target. The butts were moved still farther off – so far now that they were scarcely in sight.

As the French knight took aim, a silly lady in the stands jumped up and waved to him for luck. It spoiled his concentration and the arrow went wide.

But the sergeant-at-arms fired the perfect shot. His arrow hit the gold dead centre. Even the Saxon crowds gasped with admiration and began to turn away. The contest was plainly over.

The old man congratulated the sergeant, who jeered at him. The nobles in the stand were rising and stretching themselves, stiff after so much sitting. The old man took a green-tipped arrow from his basket and laid it to his bow. "I'll just see what I can manage," he quavered.

His arrow flew like a hornet. The thwack, as it hit canvas, sounded like an explosive charge. It pierced the selfsame hole as the sergeant's arrow, and dislodged it, leaving only one arrow thrumming with the force of impact.

"Did you see that?"

"Why? What happened?"

"He did it! Old Grandpa did it!"

The noblemen muttered and mumbled uneasily. As the old man approached, twisted and limping, to receive his prize, Prince John pointedly turned his back.

Guy of Gisborne picked up the golden arrow between finger and thumb and dropped it at the vagrant's feet. "You shoot quite well, old man," he said grudgingly, but there was no reply. He saw that the archer's face was turned not towards him but towards the Lady Marian. The mouth was hidden by the bird's nest beard but the eyes were wrinkled with smiling. And the Lady Marian was smiling back!

"Well done, sir! Oh, well done!" she said.

"You are kind, beautiful maiden, past all my deserving," said the winner.

Now you ought to know that Sir Guy of Gisborne thought of the Lady Marian as his future bride (even though she did not care for the idea). He was furious to see her smiles wasted on a filthy, doddering Saxon. He took hold of the shaggy beard to yank the rogue's head round to face him. The beard came away in his hand. The archer sank his teeth into Gisborne's clenched fist, then sprang backwards.

It was as if he had left his old age in Gisborne's grasp and been restored to youth. There stood a handsome youngster, straight-backed, bright-eyed and laughing.

"*Robin Hood!*" breathed Gisborne and for a moment the two men looked at one another with bitterest hatred.

Then a voice in the crowd shouted, "Here, Robin! Over here!" A riderless horse, slapped on the rump, galloped towards the pavilion. Robin leapt into the saddle. The flying stirrups struck the faces of the guards who tried to stop him.

Gisborne was first to mount up and give chase, while Marian crammed her long plaits against her mouth and gazed after them. "Oh, ride, Robin, ride!" she whispered under her breath. She alone among the spectators had recognised Robin Hood beneath his disguise – but then she was in love with him, and he with her.

The crowds scattered from in front of the galloping horses, as Gisborne pursued Robin towards the castle drawbridge. The golden arrow shone in Robin's hand. A cry rose from the beggars and children by the gate: "Ride, Robin! Ride!"

But Gisborne was close behind, sword drawn, and mounted on a splendid stallion, whereas Robin's horse was a poor thing. His disguise allowed for no weapon; a longbow cannot be used in the saddle.

"I've a score to settle with you, you thief!" panted Gisborne, and the blade of his sword sliced the green feathers from Robin's arrows. "You've robbed my tax gatherers, stirred up the peasants, and thumbed your nose at me out of the greenwood tree! Well, now I'll show that scum of yours that their magic Robin Hood is nothing but common flesh and blood!" This time his blade shaved the hair from Robin's neck. They thundered over the castle drawbridge side by side.

"And I have a score of scores to settle with you, Gisborne!" panted Robin. "You robbed me of my father's land. You tread down the poor and make widows and orphans weep! You drove me to live like an animal in the greenwood…"

Gisborne swung, and Robin reeled at the blow but he was not silenced: "…*when everyone knows that you are the animal!*" He turned in the saddle and struck out, using the only weapon he had.

Watching from the castle yard, the crowds saw the two horses gallop out of town, and feared for the poor man who had woken Gisborne's fury.

A short while later, the bully's horse galloped back down the streets of Nottingham, reins dangling, foamy with sweat, hooves skidding on the cobbles. Shopkeepers and housewives drew back fearfully against the walls. Then one by one they stepped out again. The horse had stopped, and stood kicking its hooves against the ground, snorting. Now the people recognised the splendid beast. It was Guy of Gisborne's horse. But the horse's saddle was empty. The rider was gone. Gisborne would never blight their lives again.

Greater **tyrants** remained: tyrants who made Gisborne seem like a gentleman. Until the true King of England returned, his subjects would continue to groan and suffer at the hands of Prince John and his robber barons. Only the existence of Robin Hood – out there – dressed like spring among the greenwood trees – kept poor people from despair. The mere mention of Robin's name kept their hearts beating. The telling of his thousand daring deeds warmed them even when there was no fuel on the hearth. In the depths of a cruel winter, Robin was the green promise that spring always returns.

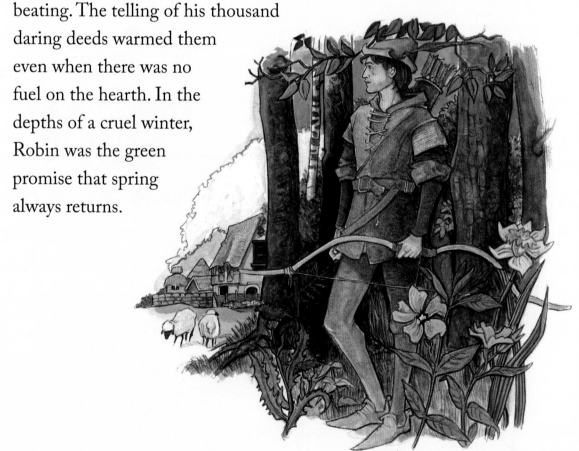

The Sherwood Bugle

HOOD GANG BEHIND GOLD THEFT?

Brave soldiers are this morning scouring Sherwood Forest in search of a band of desperate thieves who carried out an outrageous daylight ambush and then vanished into dense woodland.

The heavily protected convoy, on its way to deliver gold and jewels to the castle of our much-loved local leader, His Excellency the Sheriff of Nottingham, was intercepted at 6.35 p.m. by a group of cowardly, armed criminals, who overpowered the guards before making off with the entire cargo. According to one wounded guard the gang, all dressed in green, were well-drilled and appeared to be under the command of a mysterious hooded figure carrying a longbow.

TERROR

There can be little doubt that the raid was the work of the notorious

Robin Hood gang which has terrorised the local population for the past three years. The gang has repeatedly shown that they will stop at nothing in their efforts to disrupt the peace and harmony that our great Prince John has worked so hard to develop since he …

GOOD DAY!

The tiny village of Locksley could soon be the scene of the wedding of the century. Our reliable sources suggest that the hunky he-man outlaw Robin Hood has popped the question to his long-time girlfriend the Lady Marian, and the answer was a definite

"Yes Yes Yes!"

But could mild, meek Marian tame our rugged Robin, or is this yet another society marriage that's doomed to end up in the divorce courts (or at the end of a hangman's rope!) sooner than you can say "wanted poster"? We'll keep you posted, and rest assured, if and when the happy day arrives, you'll see those wedding photos first in *Good Day!*

EXCLUSIVE PHOTOS

ROBIN AND MARIAN TO WED?

Meanwhile, if you want to be as fit as our Robin and squeeze into that suit of armour you were ready to take down to the dump, why not try **FRIAR TUCK'S AMAZING ROAST VENISON DIET.** Shed those pounds and give your horse a break! **See page 24 for details.**

TV Interview

Presenter: ...and now over to our East Midlands correspondent, Will Weaver.

Will: Thanks, Percival. Well, rumours have been flying around Nottinghamshire regarding Robin of Locksley. Today we can clear them up, as Robin has agreed to meet us in a secret Sherwood location. Robin, what our viewers want to understand is why you think it's acceptable to steal.

Robin: Look. It's been three years since Prince John came to rule over our country. Since then this once proud nation's become a divided land, full of rich, robbing barons and poor, exploited peasants!

Will: An interesting point of view, Mr Hood, but you haven't answered my question. Stealing? How can you defend it?

Robin: Well, a lot's been written about me recently, and a lot of it deeply hurtful. I want to set the record straight.

Will: Now's your chance. Please do answer the question.

Robin: Well, as regards the accusations that my firm's activities have had a harmful effect on the good people of Nottinghamshire, it's absolute nonsense. I set up *Merrie Men Ltd* to improve the lives of the local population.

Will: But it's been rumoured that you were responsible for ambushing the Sheriff's gold convoy and wounding one of his men. How does that improve local lives?

Robin: It's never been proved that my group ambushed the gold convoy. Never. If we were to do something like that, we'd only use force as a last resort. I can assure you that all the money that comes into our possession goes straight to the poor!

Will: Let's turn to more pleasant matters. An article in *Good Day!* magazine revealed that you have asked Lady "Maid" Marian to marry you. Are wedding bells going to be ringing?

Robin: Lady Marian and I have never discussed marriage.

Will: Our viewers will be very sorry to hear that. However, she has been spotted wearing a large diamond ring on her left hand. This has nothing to do with you?

Robin: Marian and I are just good friends.

Will: One more thing, Mr Hood. A local paper has published photos of a hooded man in green leaving the Friar's Fish Restaurant with Lady Marian and she was holding a copy of *Wonderful Weddings* magazine. What do you say to that?

Robin: I say he's a lucky man. I wish him all the very best.

Will: Thank you, Mr Hood. Well, viewers – if you want to have your say on this – our phone lines are now open.

Rabbit in Mixer Survives

"Tell us a story Grandad"
The bunny rabbits implored
"About the block of concrete
Out of which you clawed."

"Tell every gory detail
Of how you struggled free
From the teeth of the Iron Monster
And swam through a quicksand sea."

"How you battled with the Humans
(And the part we like the most)
Your escape from the raging fire
When they held you there to roast."

The old adventurer smiled
And waved a wrinkled paw
"All right children, settle down,
I'll tell it just once more."

His thin nose started twitching
Near-blind eyes began to flood
As the part that doesn't age
Drifted back to bunnyhood.

When spring was king of the seasons
And days were built to last
When thunder was merely thunder
Not a distant quarry blast.

18

How, leaving the warren one morning
Looking for somewhere to play,
He'd wandered into the woods
And there had lost his way.

When suddenly without warning
The earth gave way, and he fell
Off the very edge of the world
Into the darkness of Hell.

Sharp as the colour of a carrot
On a new-born bunny's tongue
Was the picture he recalled
Of that day when he was young.

Trance-formed now by the memory
His voice was close to tears
But the story he was telling
Was falling on deaf ears.

There was giggling and nudging
And lots of "Sssh – he'll hear"
For it was a trick, a game they played
Grown crueller with each year.

"Poor old Grandad" they tittered
As they one by one withdrew
"He's told it all so often
He now believes it's true."

Young rabbits need fresh carrots
And his had long grown stale
So they left the old campaigner
Imprisoned in his tale.

Petrified by memories
Haunting ever strong
Encased in a block of time
Eighteen inches long.

Roger McGough

Should Humans *Really* Rule the Earth?

The time has come for humans to hand over the running of this planet to someone more capable.

World wars that claim millions of lives; the destruction of the rainforest; global warming; famine, tyranny and terrorism. All of this points to the conclusion that rather than running the Earth, humans are doing a great job of *ruining* it.

In their defence, humans will point to the many ways in which they *believe* they're superior to other creatures:

1 They'll argue that their social structure is much more sophisticated than any other species. Elephants, however, appear to exist in social groups as clearly defined as humans, and demonstrate bonds just as strong as human family ties, working together to take care of weaker members of the tribe.

2 Humans like to pride themselves on their athletic prowess, drooling over gold medal performances at the Olympic Games, but the fastest human sprinter, reaching speeds of 23 miles per hour, would be left way behind by the pace of a cheetah: a staggering 70 miles per hour!

3 Human children are really special though, aren't they? Go into any nursery and watch them painting pictures and learning games. However, when faced with the question: "Could they cope on their own?" the answer is of course "No"! A human child depends entirely on adults until aged four or five. Baby loggerhead sea turtles, on the other hand, are left to fend for themselves as soon as they're born. Then they immediately embark on a 9,000 mile migration across the Atlantic Ocean.

4 However, surely humans are the most intelligent species on the planet? Well, that may be true, but if so why do they often forget where they've put their car keys? Compare that with migrating birds which can cover thousands of miles over oceans and mountains to locate the very rock where they nested last year. Furthermore, they do all this without a map or satnav!

Admittedly, there are valid points that humans can use to support their case. They can be proud of:

- Putting a man on the Moon
- Establishing a worldwide Internet
- The masterworks of writers and composers such as Shakespeare or Beethoven.

Certainly it's difficult to imagine snails, camels or goldfish reaching such achievements.

Nevertheless, my argument is that it's this relentless pursuit of "progress" which is actually damaging society and the environment. It's time to embrace the simpler life. Hand over control now, humans, before it's too late!

Animals Rule! ...But Which One?

If humans really were to step down, who *should* be given the job of running this planet? We invited all creatures to put forward their case to be made Rulers of the Earth. Here are the five finalists (translated into Human English to make it easier for you to read):

Apes

It's been widely reported that humans evolved from us apes (which all apes see as an insult, by the way). Therefore, once humans have gone we should be left in charge. Having learned from their mistakes, by the time we've evolved into humans again we'll be ideally prepared to make a much better job of it next time round.

VOTE APE

Flies

One look at the figures should tell you why flies should rule the world. There are billions and billions of us. If there was an election tomorrow we'd win it ~~hands~~ wings down. Additionally, if anybody gets in our way we can easily spread some kind of horrid disease to kill them off.

VOTE FLY

Lions

Excuse me, but which beast is referred to as "King of the Jungle"? There's a reason for that, you know. It's because we're bigger and tougher than any other animal. Who'd dare take us on in a fight to be Number One? A fly? Don't think so, and an ape would just run away making screeching noises. We'll be the next rulers, make no mistake.

VOTE LION

Peacocks

Hey, slow down a minute, cat. Why this obsession with power and fighting? As everybody knows, the most attractive feature of any creature is their appearance, and who can match us? We'd spread joy throughout the land. Vote Peacock for Peace, man!

VOTE PEACOCK

Bees

I think you're missing a crucial point here guys. What do we all need to survive? Oxygen, right? And where does it come from? You got it: plants! And who pollinates those plants to make sure there's enough of them to keep the oxygen supply going? Us bees, that's who. Without us you'd be finished.

VOTE BEE

So that's all five finalists, now it's time to cast your vote: which creature *should* rule the world instead of humans? Pick up your phones – the lines are now open!

PEOPLE POWER!

Tigers roaming the streets of London?
Wild dog packs hunting down your pets?
The fear of leaving your house after dark?
Is that what you want?
Stop this nonsense now!

Vote **PEOPLE POWER**
for law and order

ANIMAL RULE!

Fellow creatures!
What have humans done for us?
- Stuck us in cages to be gawped at.
- Massacred us for food, furs, skins, tusks or horns.

Enough! It's time for a return to the natural order.

Vote **ANIMAL RULE**

Brashem's Tortoise

Susan Price

"Shop, Brashem!"

In the smelly cave of the shop, the parrot **scuttled** sideways on its perch, squawking. It spread its red and blue wings, arched its tail and sent sunflower seeds flying. In the dimness its bright colours glowed like half-lit jewels.

Other shops had brass bells behind the door to jangle when you went in, but Brashem had a parrot. Every customer through the door shouted, "Shop, Brashem!" and the parrot had learned it from them. Some customers still shouted for Brashem, out of habit, but they didn't need to anymore. The parrot shouted for them.

Jessie Hanrahan peered round, to see if Brashem **lurked** in a shadowy corner. She clutched a tortoise tightly to her chest. There was nothing to see of the tortoise except its shell. It had pulled its head and legs inside.

"Put it down, and let's go," Olive Tromans said. Olive was frightened of Brashem, who owned a shop and was an important person.

"We've got to give it to her," Jessie said. She wasn't shy, and she loved the shop. When you opened the door, it breathed in your face, with whiffs of dry dust, wet mud and violet cashews. As you moved round inside, the smells changed: now a smell of sharp cheese, then a **reek** of carbolic soap, that changed to a sickly stink of paraffin.

Even on the sunniest of days, it was dark inside the shop because the windows were blocked with long strings of cardboard packets holding hair-pins and hair-nets, combs, buttons, pins and needles, packs of cards, pencils and cotton-reels, candles, boot-laces. And things never sold now, such as button-hooks, fly-papers, wash-boards, and sheets of sweet-scented "Snowfire" face-powder, for ladies to press on their noses.

The parrot spread its glowing wings. A parrot wouldn't be allowed in a shop selling food these days, but this was 1938. People were tough then. They didn't care about a few parrot-germs.

Jessie called, "Mrs Brashem!"

The parrot leaned from its perch, turning its head sideways to see her. It squawked, "Coming!" Jessie longed to touch its soft, bright feathers but was afraid of its big beak. Olive kept well away from it.

The shop wasn't like a modern shop. It was a little terraced house, like the others in the street, and Brashem had turned the front room into her business.

The cash-register stood on the end of the sideboard. In front of the sideboard grey sacks slumped, gaping open to show their contents: potatoes, carrots, turnips, peas in their shells – whatever was in season. They always had dirt from the fields still on them, and it made the bare floorboards muddy, and gave the shop a smell of earth.

A big wooden table, an old kitchen table, held a set of iron scales, with a scoop. Its weights were piled beside it. A whole joint of cooked beef covered in muslin lay across the table. Jessie always thought it looked spooky, like a body wrapped in a shroud. Of course it did – a cow's body.

The dimness at the back of the shop was the girls' favourite place, the treasure cave. A tall, heavy dresser towered to the ceiling, its every shelf packed with glistening glass jars of jewels. Emerald green and topaz-yellow acid-drops. Ruby red kisses, shaped like lips. Heart-shaped violet cashews, pale amethysts, to scent your breath. Green peppermints. Coconut mushrooms. Gobstoppers that changed colour as you sucked them – some so enormous you could hardly force your mouth wide enough to cram them past your teeth.

Olive edged over to stand by Jessie and stare at the sweets. They longed for them. They yearned for the bright colours, the sugary smell, the **luscious** tastes. When they had sweets, they hoarded them for days, opening the paper bag to admire the colours, and sniff the scent. They'd give one a few licks, just to taste it, and then put it back. They made sweets last days, because it was always so long before they had more.

Brashem burst from her back room with the slam of a door, and the parrot scuttled along its perch, screeching, "Nice day!"

"We found your tortoise, Mrs Brashem!" Jessie held the tortoise up. "He was running away down the street! So I thought we'd better bring him back."

"He was legging it down the street!" Brashem said. "How can I thank you for recapturing him? Should you like some sweets?"

The girls looked at each other. They couldn't speak. Dumbly, they gazed at Brashem, and nodded.

Brashem, the Keeper of the Treasure, went over to the tower of gleaming jars. "What should you like?"

Olive chose a gobstopper nearly as big as her fist. Jessie asked for a coconut mushroom, a red kiss, and a badger-striped humbug. Brashem put them into flimsy white paper bags, and the girls waltzed from the shop like millionairesses leaving the Ritz.

A week later, they were back in the shop. This time, Olive held the tortoise, though she was still too shy to speak.

"What, did he escape again?" Brashem said. She was weighing potatoes for Mrs Riley, who sat on a kitchen chair beside the table, holding her shopping bag on her lap. The parrot strutted on his perch and screamed, "King Edward's!"

"He was right down the end of the street," Jessie said. "A cart could have run over him."

"What do you think, Mrs Riley? Do they deserve a reward for rescuing my tortoise from the jaws of death?"

"They do, Mrs Brashem."

"I wonder, what should it be?"

"A bit of that sharp cheese, Mrs Brashem. Good enough for the King, your sharp cheese."

Brashem looked at Jessie and Olive. "Should you like a bit of sharp cheese?"

Jessie felt her face **grimacing**, and tried hard to keep it straight. "No, thank you, Mrs Brashem."

"Well, bless me, I can't think what you'd want, then. A button hook?"

"No, thank you, Mrs Brashem."

"A packet of Beecham's Pills?"

Olive, looking at her shoe's toe, and blushing, said, "Some sweets, please, Mrs Brashem."

"Sweets? Really?" Brashem sounded so astonished that Jessie guessed she was laughing at them. "Sweets are no use."

"A scrubbing brush is very useful," Mrs Riley said.

Jessie grinned. "Could we have sweets, please, Mrs Brashem?"

"No accounting for taste," Brashem said. "Come and choose some, then."

Olive put the tortoise down on the grey floor boards. It lay there, hidden inside its shell. Mrs Riley paid for her shopping, and left. The parrot screamed, "Goodbye!"

"A red lollipop, please," Jessie said.

"Some dolly-mixtures, please," said Olive, and Brashem gave her a handful of the tiny, bead-like sweets.

Outside, they beamed at each other. "Easy-peasy!" Jessie said.

"It's only been two days since last time," Olive said. "She'll know it's us."

"Tortoises escape all the time," Jessie said.

"No, they don't. They can't climb. Or fly."

"Do you want a quarter of love-hearts or what?" Jessie said.

"We'll get into trouble," Olive said.

"Why? We're helping. And I bet that tortoise gets fed up, stuck in that little yard. Go and make sure Brashem's in the shop."

Olive trotted down the entry to the street, and peeped into Brashem's shop. The parrot, shuffling on its perch, tilted its head and eyed her sidelong. Then an old man went in, and the parrot screamed for Brashem. Olive ran back to the entry and waved to Jessie at its other end.

Jessie was in the yard behind the street of houses, standing by the gate of Brashem's little garden. She shoved the gate wide, dived in, snatched up the tortoise and quickly left the yard again, slamming the gate behind her.

At the end of the entry, she tried to hand the tortoise to Olive. "No, your turn!" Olive said.

"Cowardy custard!"

"Don't care!" Olive said. "My mum saw me with it last time."

"What did you tell her?"

"Nothing!" Olive said. "But I'm not having it again."

Jessie took the tortoise home. Their yard was thick with dandelions. She picked a big handful of leaves, sat on her doorstep, and held the leaves by its shell until the tortoise emerged and nibbled.

Brashem was less and less grateful every time they took the tortoise back. Last time, she'd only given them one small lollipop each.

Perhaps they should keep the tortoise until the next morning? Brashem would miss it overnight, and be worried. Then she'd be more grateful when they returned it. She might even give them a whole quarter of sweets each.

Jessie daydreamed about what sweets she would choose. Jaw-breaker toffees? Ju-jubes? Aniseed balls?

"What are you doing with that thing?"

Jessie jumped. The harsh voice was her mother's, and there was her mother, tall and thin, standing over her. Clutching the tortoise, Jessie jumped to her feet. Her mother never usually came home this early.

"That thing belongs to Brashem," her mother said.

"I found it!" Jessie said. "I'm taking it back but I thought I should give it something to eat first." She looked up at her mother, willing her to believe.

Mrs Hanrahan said, "Mrs Tromans told me that Olive had that thing the other day."

"Did she?" Jessie's voice had gone high and squeaky.

"She said Brashem gave Olive some sweets for taking it back."

"Did she?" Olive hadn't been telling the truth when she'd said she'd told her mother "nothing".

Jessie's mother glowered down at her. "I think we'll go and see Brashem."

"No need!" Jessie cried.

"I'll hurry up and take it back! I— "

Jessie's mother raised her eyebrows and Jessie knew better than to argue any more.

Hugging the tortoise, and feeling shaky and near to tears, Jessie walked in front of her mother, like a prisoner being marched to punishment. They passed Olive's house. Olive was outside, playing with one of her little sisters. When she saw Jessie, with the tortoise, and her mother, she jumped up and looked ready to dash back into her house.

"Oh, yes, Olive Tromans," Jessie's mother said. "Feeling guilty, are you? I think you should come with us too."

In those days, you did what adults told you, whether they were your mother or not. Olive looked miserable, but she joined the prisoners' march. They pulled faces at each other, trying to guess what it would be safe to say.

They stopped at the shop's door, but Jessie's mother reached over their heads and pushed it open. The parrot shrieked, "Shop, Brashem!"

Jessie hoped that Brashem was out – but Brashem came out of the back. She never went out.

"Brashem," Jessie's mother said, "I think this pair have been playing tricks on you."

"What, Jessie and Olive?" Brashem said. "They never would."

"I know my daughter," said Mrs Hanrahan. "They've been stealing your tortoise and bringing it back for a reward."

"Oh no," Brashem said. "It got out under my gate. Just the twice. I shall block that gate off when I remember."

"Just the twice," Mrs Hanrahan repeated heavily.

"Oh yes. Today – and a week ago. I gave 'em a few sweets for being good girls. Where's the harm?"

"Just the twice," Mrs. Hanrahan said.

"Only today and a week ago," Jessie said, looking up at her mother. She tried to make her eyes big and sweet. Her mother's face relaxed a little, and Jessie laughed inside herself. Her mother was going to believe them!

The parrot lifted its wings, flirted its tail, and screamed, "Brought that tortoise back again!"

Mrs Hanrahan looked from the parrot to Brashem, and then down at the girls. She folded her arms.

"Reward you with sweets!" squawked the parrot.

"Only twice, eh?" Mrs Hanrahan said. "That parrot must be a quick learner."

Jessie was surprised to see Brashem's face turning red as a post-box. She'd never seen an adult blush before.

"I'll thank you not to encourage my daughter and her friend to lie and cheat," Mrs Hanrahan said.

"A few sweets," Brashem said. "It was lovely to see their little faces. Where was the harm?"

"It's your shop," Mrs Hanrahan said. "If you want to give your stock away for nothing, that's your business. Ah, but you won't do that, will you, because then you'd have every child in the neighbourhood in here, holding its hand out. So you play this little game with the tortoise – very funny to you. But you're teaching these girls to steal and lie to get what they want instead of working for it. I don't take kindly to that, Mrs Brashem. It's hard enough to bring a child up on the straight and narrow as it is."

"Mrs Hanrahan – I don't know what to say."

"You can say you won't give any more sweets to these two."

Brashem looked apologetically at Jessie and Olive. "I won't. I promise."

"Good. Now, Jessie, give the tortoise back and say you're sorry."

Jessie handed the tortoise back to Brashem, and she and Olive **snivelled**, "Sorry."

Mrs Hanrahan turned to go.

"Mrs Hanrahan," Brashem called after her. "If Jessie and Olive gathered leaves for me – and tidied the yard up – and did little jobs – would it be all right if I paid 'em in sweets then?"

Mrs Hanrahan considered, then nodded. "If they're working for the sweets, yes."

Brashem smiled, and Jessie and Olive smiled back. "Come and see me tomorrow. Can you blacklead a range?"

The girls nodded, but not happily. Polishing a cooking-range with black lead was hard, dirty work.

"They should get a whole quarter of sweets for that," Mrs Hanrahan said, and Brashem nodded.

Jessie and Olive grinned. A whole quarter of sweets! "Can we choose what kind?" Jessie asked.

"Anything you like, if you do a good job."

Their smiles were even wider. Blackleading wasn't so bad if there was a quarter of barley sugars at the end.

"See you tomorrow," Brashem called as Mrs Hanrahan opened the door.

The parrot screamed, "Goodbye! See you later!"

◀ ▶ ⬆

Home   About   Advice   Articles

Exotic Pets

Email sign-up

Enter your email address

Current eNews

The Facts and Figures

The trade in exotic pets is estimated to be worth up to £4 billion worldwide. The list of animals classed as "exotic" pets is constantly being amended as fashions change. Amongst the more common pets now classed as exotic are:

- alligators
- wolves
- tigers
- tortoises
- chinchillas
- parrots
- hedgehogs
- snakes
- lizards
- primates such as chimpanzees.

News   **Links**   **Contact us**   **Search**

The Facts

1 Germany is the biggest importer of exotic pets in Europe, followed by Spain, France, and the UK. It is thought that there may be as many as 1,000 different types of exotic pet in the UK.

2 In 2006, Europe introduced the <u>Wild Bird Import Ban</u>. This resulted in an increase in the import of reptiles such as lizards and snakes instead of birds.

3 A baby chimp can cost as much as £30,000.

4 A tiger cub can be bought for as little as £300 in some countries, but when fully grown its food bill could reach £600 per month!

5 Police in California have seized deer, mountain lions and even bears being kept illegally as pets.

6 There are an estimated 5,000 tigers living in the wild today and over 5,000 living as pets in the USA.

7 Up to 80% of birds and reptiles traded illegally do not survive the capture and transportation process.

Home   About   Advice   Articles

Exotic Pets

Are You Sure You Really Want One?

It may seem like a good idea at the time...

Wow, did you see the way its tongue shot out to catch that fly?

Look at that baby chimp with its big round eyes. I want to cuddle him.

I love its brightly-coloured feathers. I'm going to train it to say my name!

...but are you properly equipped to keep an exotic pet?

Before buying, there are several important points that need to be considered.

1 **Legal issues:** there are laws and restrictions on the import and trade of exotic pets. Some types of exotic pet may be banned. All proper documentation should be obtained and checked before purchase.

2 **Environment:** exotic pets will probably have very different demands from pets such as cats, dogs and rabbits. A suitable environment needs to be created, either indoors or outdoors, which will allow the creature to exercise freely. Temperature and levels of sunlight must be controlled – many exotic pets suffer from a deficiency of Vitamin D due to lack of sunlight.

3 **Diet:** although some exotic pets may be bought fairly cheaply, their diet may be extremely specialised and therefore expensive. Again, research is necessary before making an initial purchase.

4 **Health risks:** the behaviour of exotic pets is liable to be unpredictable. Some will never bond with humans, and can become very aggressive when fully grown. Others may bond with their owners but then become aggressive towards strangers such as friends or visitors. Diseases can be passed on through bites and scratches, and pets can also be at risk from diseases picked up from their new environment. The cost of treatment should be borne in mind too – a vet's bill is likely to be much higher than for a common household pet.

5 **Care:** many exotic pets will demand a great deal of attention and upkeep. If the owner becomes ill, goes on holiday or moves house this can cause severe complications.

Home   About   Advice   Articles

Exotic Pets

Protection of Exotic Pets Society

PEPS was founded as a charity in 2005, to protect exotic species from exploitation.

The problems:

The trade in illegal sales of exotic pets is thriving. Some countries have strict controls on imports, though unfortunately many countries lag behind. Illegal traders are prepared to forge official documentation and take advantage of slack customs procedures to smuggle animals across borders.

Dealers may be dishonest about the health risks involved and upkeep required when the animal reaches maturity. Many owners soon find themselves unable to cope with a noisy parrot, or hungry tiger.

News	Links	Contact us	Search

Donate to PEPS

Owners who can't cope with their exotic pet have two options:

1 They can return the pet to the dealer, who will probably sell it on to another owner. Many pets spend their life being passed from one unsuitable owner to another.

2 They can abandon the pet into the wild. This can have a devastating effect on both the pet and creatures native to the environment.

The answers:

✔ PEPS is lobbying governments to establish common laws on the import of exotic creatures. We also seek more severe punishments for illegal trafficking.

✔ We are demanding greater funding for Animal Controls at customs stations. Illegal animals could then be identified.

✔ We are seeking to increase awareness of the special demands involved when keeping exotic pets.

Gone Away!

Lou Kuenzler

Brendan is my best mate. At least, I think he is… I hope he is… I'm not so sure anymore.

Brendan has gone away.

After everything that happened, his family moved. They wanted to make a new beginning – to be somewhere else. Somewhere with fewer memories, I suppose.

They took Brendan with them.

"Come and see us, Leon," said Brendan's mum. "It's not very far on the train." She was smiling but her voice sounded all **hoarse** and breathy.

And I will go. I'll go soon. Really soon. But not this weekend. This weekend I'm hanging out with Sam.

* * * *

It's funny, when Brendan was still here – just round the corner – I'd stop off at his house all the time.

"D'you want to come to the shop?" I'd ask, all **nonchalant**, trying to look cool. That was important. With Brendan you couldn't seem too keen.

"No," he'd say. "But you'll bring me something back. Right?"

I think that's what Miss McVeigh, our teacher, calls a rhetorical question because we both knew I would bring him something.

Sometimes I'd get him a comic. Or a pack of football cards. Perhaps some chocolate or crisps.

Brendan's lounge always smelt of new leather sofas. He had an MP3 the size of a stamp and a TV the size of a cinema screen. My mum says his family are really "well heeled". But he never offered to pay me back. Not once!

* * * *

Sam's going to stay the night.

He can have my bed and I'll have a sleeping bag on the floor.

It's a bit embarrassing, really. I've had the same sleeping bag since I was little. It's got a big, red space rocket on it!

Sam won't laugh, though. He's cool like that. He'll just wrinkle his nose and say something funny. Something to make it a joke.

"You think that's bad!" he might say. "You should see my swimming towel. It's yellow with fluffy ducks all over it."

He probably does have a silly towel, too… or hideous slippers. Something like that.

Not Brendan. Brendan always had the latest stuff.

* * * *

Last night was excellent!

We stayed up really late watching this crazy old film in black and white. It was about a giant, **vengeful** jelly that plops out of the sky and attacks New York City.

It was so lame. Not one bit scary. But Sam and I screamed like we were being assassinated.

We really did manage to frighten ourselves — just a little. I love that… that feeling…being scared and safe all at the same time.

As the jelly oozed closer, Sam hunched up like a squirrel, protecting his face with a cage of fingers. I hid behind a cushion and peeped out.

At one bit, when the demented jelly was oozing up the Empire State Building, we screamed so loudly Dad came in.

His hair was sticking up all over the place. He looked like a bear disturbed in hibernation!

"What's going on in here, Leon?" he yawned.

"Attack of The Killer Jelly," I squealed.

Sam laughed so hard he nearly choked.

* * * *

"I had a great time," said Sam, before he left.

I had a great time too. It was one of the best sleepovers I've ever had.

I hate saying that.

Sorry, Brendan. But it's true.

* * * *

Me and Brendan had some great sleepovers of our own, though.

I remember our last one. One of the last times I saw him.

We were over at his house, sleeping in his bunk beds.

I'd love to have bunks in my room. I like the idea of always having somewhere ready in case a friend comes over to stay.

But Brendan hated them. He wanted one of those stilt beds with a computer-station underneath.

"Bunks are for kids!" he said. (Like he was so mature.)

But he wanted to sleep on the top bunk, all the same.

"Can't I?" I begged. "I always have to sleep on the bottom."

"It's my room," said Brendan.

"Exactly. You can sleep on the top bunk whenever you want." I could hear my voice going all high-pitched and whiney. I hate that. Brendan always said it made me sound like a girl. So I shrugged, "It doesn't matter."

"No!" said Brendan. "Let's make it fair. We'll toss for it. OK?"

He took a coin from his pocket.

"Heads or tails," he said.

"Tails," I said. (I'm sure I said that.
I nearly always do.)

And I was in luck! It came out tails.

But Brendan shifted the goal posts as always.
"Better make it the best of three."

After that it came up heads every time.

Brendan won.

I'm glad now that he won. Of course I am. But at the time I felt like he'd kicked me or something. It made me feel all angry and pathetic — like a dog in the dirt.

Why did you always have to **manipulate** everything, Brendan?

It's like I was a yo-yo and he had the string!

* * * *

That wasn't it.

That wasn't what was great about the sleepover...obviously not.

That's just how me and Brendan used to carry on... You know, like best mates do sometimes.

No, the funny bit was later. In the middle of the night.

I was lying there fast asleep.

Brendan said I was snoring, BUT I WAS NOT.

I was lying there when — all of a sudden — SPLOSH!

I woke up gasping, thinking I was drowning. Like in those dreams where your lungs are stone and your limbs turn concrete.

But it was only Brendan. For a laugh, he'd lent down and tipped a jug of water over me. "Sorry, Leon," he said, "I've wet the bed. Now it's dripped all over your head."

He really laughed then. He told me how he'd been planning it all day. Brendan laughed so much he nearly did wet himself. I laughed too...a bit.

It was hard to get back to sleep though. Brendan wouldn't let me go and find a dry sheet.

"Mum'll be livid," he said. "She'll go off like a Catherine wheel if she knows I've been mucking around. I promised I wouldn't do anything to you this time."

* * * *

Sam and I are going to the fair.

Just like that. No planning or anything. Brendan always had to plan trips. That way he could act like a football manager picking players for a premiership game. He'd run trials, threaten substitutions and be sure to leave someone on the bench. My trial always involved doing his maths homework for him.

"You don't have to," he'd grin. "I'd do it myself, only I have to organise the bowling trip. And you do want to come with me? Right?"

Sam doesn't go in for strategies. He just said, "Shall we go?"

And we did.

The queue for The Fall of Death was really long, so we didn't bother waiting. We both agreed we would have been brave enough. It was just that queuing was a waste of time.

We did have a go on the dodgems and the waltzer. And we went on the ghost train twice for a laugh.

After that we only had enough money left for one of us to have another ride.

"Doesn't seem fair," said Sam. "Let's put the money together and try and win something instead."

We went to one of those stalls where you can catch a goldfish.

"You throw the hoop," said Sam. "You're better at sports than me."

"But I'm rubbish at sports!" I said.

"And I'm rubbish rubbish," Sam grinned. "Olympic Gold rubbish!"

So I took the hoop. I threw it towards the middle of the stall. It wobbled a bit…dropped sideways…and landed over a bag with two fish.

We'd won!

Sam and I stood there gasping like goldfish ourselves. We couldn't believe it.

"Who's going to keep them?" I asked.

"I don't mind," said Sam. "Fairground fish always die anyway. They'll be dead in a couple of days."

Suddenly, I knew I couldn't have them. I couldn't take the fish home. Not if they were going to die.

"I don't want them," I said. And, even though I didn't explain, Sam seemed to understand right away.

"No worries!" He took the fish from me and gave them to a little girl who hadn't won.

"What's their names?" she asked.

"Bob," said Sam...

"And Brendan," I said.

I don't know why I said that. But I did.

* * * *

"You should go and see Brendan, soon," said Sam. "Spend time up there. Hang out."

We were getting ready for music club after school. Brendan wasn't into clubs. He said they weren't cool. But Sam and I joined this music thing and now I'm learning to play the guitar.

"Go and visit?" I shook my head. My stomach clenched. It was as if my guts were guitar strings and someone was twisting them tight.

"I – I can't go," I faltered. "It'd be weird."

Sam shrugged, "You'll feel better if you do, Leon. You should go next weekend. It's half term."

* * * *

On the way home, Sam and I passed Blue Notes. It's this really old music shop. There's a thin snow of dust on top of everything. Brendan would never have let us come in here. He'd have said it was cheap and second hand! But Sam likes the music they play and I like looking at the electric guitars (even though most of them are way too big for me).

We've both started a collection of plectrums – the little discs you pluck guitar strings with – so we went in to see if any new ones had arrived.

"Maybe I should take one for Brendan," I said flicking the plectrums over in their tin.

Sam looked surprised. "Did he play?"

"No," I shifted my feet, feeling awkward all of a sudden. "But it'd be nice to take something."

I remembered how I'd always brought him things from the corner shop.

"How about a badge," said Sam. "That might be good."

I looked at the collection of badges pinned to a notice board. They were mostly band names. Or pictures of instruments and musical notes.

"We never really talked about music," I said. "I don't know what he'd be in to."

"This lot are cool," said Sam. He picked up a badge with KINDRED SPIRIT written round the edge.

"Spirit? Like some kind of ghost?" I looked at Sam aghast.

But Mr Bad-Beard (that's what we call the hairy, old hippy behind the till) chipped in. "Don't you learn anything at school?" he said. "A kindred spirit's not a ghost. It means you're on the same wave length as someone else. You think the same way about things."

"That's not me and Brendan, then," I laughed. "We don't... didn't... think the same way about anything. When he was here, Brendan was always saying that I was an alien space-cake! Half the time he didn't get what was going on with me at all."

Sam frowned, his open face serious and clouded for once.

"That was his loss," he scowled. "I think Brendan treated you like dirt. I know I shouldn't say anything bad about him, but..."

"He was all right!" I snapped. "He was my mate…"

I didn't want to hear what Sam was saying. I didn't want to think. I just wanted to find something to take to Brendan.

Sam shrugged, "How about this, then?" He held up a badge with a bird on it. The bird was some kind of hawk. It had its wings spread, gliding towards the horizon. It was silver and black. The most expensive badge on the board.

"Perfect," I said. "He'd love that."

* * * *

I did visit Brendan — at long last — after all this time.

At first, I didn't know what to say. I just stood there. Awkward. Staring.

"I'm sorry," I said at last. "I'm sorry I wasn't the friend you wanted me to be."

And then I said it all. Everything.

I said how angry he'd made me sometimes…how small he'd made me feel. And I told him about how Sam and I hung around together now.

Tears were streaming down my face. That was the worst thing of all. If Brendan had seen me cry, he'd have called me a baby. "A little baby girl!"

"But I don't care," I told him. "You're my mate and I miss you. I miss you every single day… I don't understand why you had to go away."

The leaves rustled in the trees behind me. I stood up and looked down at where Brendan lay — at his grey, rain-coloured gravestone. The only splash of colour was his team's football flag fluttering in the wind.

I felt in my pocket for the badge and, clipping the bird to the edge of the flag, I watched as it fluttered in the wind.

"You've gone now, Brendan," I whispered. "You've gone away."

I felt tired and empty, then — like I'd been kicked hard in the stomach. There was nothing left in me. No more to say.

I turned and walked back through the graveyard.

* * * *

Sam came round the next day.

I must have looked a bit **forlorn** because he said: "Don't worry about it. You can still be Brendan's best mate... but I like hanging out with you, too. If that's OK."

"Sure!" I said, trying to sound nonchalant. But it doesn't really matter what you say with Sam. I don't always have to be cool.

It's because we're kindred spirits, I suppose.

Alexander Selkirk
Biography

Birth Certificate

Surname: Selkirk

Christian Name: Alexander

Date of Birth: 12th day of August, the year of our Lord 1676

Place of Birth: Parish of Lower Largo, in the county of Fife, Scotland

Father's Profession: Cobbler and Tanner

Accounts suggest that the young Alexander Selkirk was a badly behaved child who did not enjoy village life. Forced into drinking sea water by his elder brother, Alex somehow "disgraced himself" in church resulting in a summons to appear at the local court. Not willing to face any punishment, Selkirk ran away to sea. He proved himself a skilled seaman and was taken on as First Mate on the ship *Cinque Ports*. Predictably his relations with the crew and Captain gradually disintegrated, until their parting in unfortunate circumstances.

Ship's Log, 23 September, 1704

Following his persistent and vociferous complaints regarding the safety of this vessel, I yesterday put ashore Sailing Master Alexander Selkirk on the island of Mas a Tierra, off the coast of Chile. It was with relief that we watched his figure disappear over the horizon, as he has been a frequent cause of disharmony. He was abandoned with his belongings.

William Dampier, Captain, *Cinque Ports*

Home   Articles   Links   Contact Us

Alexander Selkirk

Early life

Piracy

Castaway

Old Age

Castaway

Selkirk immediately regretted his request to be put ashore. He'd hoped to persuade others to follow, but finding himself alone he ran along the beach, trying to get the ship to come back for him. When that didn't happen he settled down to wait for the next passing ship to appear. After many days it became clear that rescue was far from certain, so he began to settle into island life.

Living at first on the beach on a diet of shellfish, he soon ventured into the interior to hunt for food, which he found in the form of goats. On one occasion he chased a goat over the edge of a cliff, and though he was lucky enough to land on the beast he lay there unconscious for what he believes to have been a whole day. He made the goats' woolly skins into clothes to keep him warm and dry.

He used his tools to cut down trees and build a hut, slowly forging a bond with the wild cats which were attracted by the warmth and light of his camp fire. They kept the rats away as he slept.

Years passed, until one day he looked out to see the masts of two ships in the bay. Racing out to meet his rescuers he realised just in time that the ships belonged to the hostile Spanish navy. He fled into the dense forest until they'd sailed away.

Search

Salvation finally arrived on 2 February 1709 when two British <u>privateers</u> anchored in the bay. He was saved at last! Incredibly, the captain of one of the ships was his old captain aboard from the *Cinque Ports*, William Dampier. From him he learned just how wise a decision deserting the ship had been. Only months after dropping Selkirk off on his island, the *Cinque Ports* had sunk, with only the captain and a few men surviving.

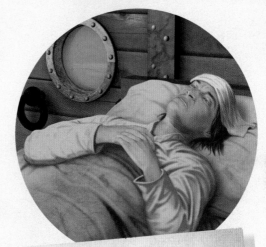

Selkirk's adventures as a castaway are thought to be the inspiration for <u>Daniel Defoe</u>'s novel <u>Robinson Crusoe</u>.

January 29 1722

Dear John,

It was with great sadness that I learnt yesterday of the death of my brother Alex. It appears he took fever in December whilst at sea, and his body was commended to the deep. After returning to us a rich man, we had hoped that he would remain with his family in Fife, but alas his was a character not to be confined by village life, and he decided to resume his successful career as Ship's Captain. We shall miss him greatly.

The Elephant in the Room

Lou Kuenzler

Characters

Lina Chang – a 12-year-old schoolgirl

Caitlin – a girl in Lina's class

Mr Chang – Lina's father

The Elephant – an oppressive presence in the room

The action takes place in the present day in Southampton (a city on the south coast of England). Lina lives with her parents in a flat overlooking the sea.

Scene 1

Late Friday afternoon. A bus stop in the town centre. Caitlin is holding a small carrier bag and keeps looking excitedly inside at what she has bought. Lina is pacing up and down, clearly anxious.

Lina	You said this wouldn't take long, Caitlin! You said we wouldn't be late.
Caitlin	Relax! The bus will be here any minute. Anyway, we're not late. It's only half past.

Lina checks her watch.

Lina	Rubbish. It's nearly quarter to already!
Caitlin	So what! It's Friday night! It's not like we've got to do our homework straight away or anything. You're such a goodie-two-shoes, you are! I bet you just want to get home and do your science project or something.
Lina	No...

Caitlin is jumping up and down clapping her hands. It is obvious she thinks she is being really funny.

Caitlin	Oh, come on! I know I'm right! I bet it's because you want to draw little bug pictures and label them. I bet you're going to make up special graphs and charts and colour them all in perfectly.
Lina	No...
Caitlin	I'm doing my project with Bella. I'm going round to her house on Sunday. Who are you doing your project with?
Lina	Nobody.
Caitlin	How come? Didn't anyone want to?
Lina	It's just easier to work on my own...unless it's at school.
Caitlin	Our project is about dragonflies and Bella's found this really cool website, so it'll only take about two minutes to find all the information. What's yours going to be about?
Lina	(*Looks at her shoes.*) I don't know. Earthworms, maybe.
Caitlin	Earthworms! (*She laughs as if she's going to burst.*) Yuk! THAT IS SO FUNNY!

Lina	I didn't choose it. Mr Hartwell said I should… He said earthworms are actually quite interesting!
Caitlin	(*Snorts.*) You've got to admit that is funny? It's SO perfect for you, Lina. You're just like an earthworm, you are. Always shut away in the dark. Never doing anything. Never going anywhere.
Lina	I do go places! I go to school, don't I? And I'm here with you now, just because you wanted to buy earrings!
Caitlin	I mean *proper* places. In the holidays and at weekends. You always just stay at home with your mum and dad.
Lina	Actually, you're wrong! My mum's never there. She works at the hospital every weekend. And in the evenings, too. The wards don't just close so everyone can go to the cinema or have a picnic, you know! And it's better if Mum works when I'm home because… Well, it's just easier that's all.
Caitlin	All right, there's no need to be touchy! But you do stay home with your dad all the time. He never goes anywhere. Bella reckons he's aerobic or something. Is that right? A friend of Bella's auntie had the same thing.
Lina	(*Mumbles under her breath.*) Agoraphobic…
Caitlin	What?
Lina	Nothing. I just said, no. He's not aerobic. (*Lina smiles – but not a happy smile – more as if she is really tired.*) Aerobic means when you jump up and down to exercise – like in a fitness class or dancing.
Caitlin	I can't imagine your dad dancing!
Lina	No! (*She laughs.*) But I think he used to.
Caitlin	Not like me, though! I'm going to dance all weekend. I've got my Drama Club show tomorrow afternoon – we're doing a musical and we dance to these really crazy old rock and

roll songs. You should try and get a ticket. It's so funny. Then there's Tanya's birthday disco on Saturday night. Are you coming to that or not?

Lina shakes her head.

Caitlin   (*Barely seeming to notice.*) I'm going to wear my new jeans with my blue top and (*she blows a kiss into the shopping bag*) that's why I got you, my beautiful little earrings. You are going to sparkle under the lights!

Lina has to laugh.

Lina   You'll look gorgeous in them. (*Caitlin holds the earrings up against herself.*) They're all shiny … like a dragonfly!

Caitlin   (*Gives Lina a hug.*) Thank you. And thanks for coming to get them with me. I'm not allowed into town on my own.

Lina   That's OK. But I do wish the bus would come. I really have to get home now. (*She checks her watch again.*) My mum left for work fifteen minutes ago. Dad'll be all on his own.

Caitlin   What's the big deal? My dad loves being on his own. He watches sport on telly and puts his feet up on the settee. (*But then she looks at her watch too.*) Oh no. It is taking ages. If I'm late for supper my mum'll kill me!

Lina   (*Under her breath*) And if I'm late my dad'll do something terrible.

Scene 2

Lina is home at last. She opens the door to the small flat and comes into the living room. She throws her backpack on the floor.

Lina	(*Calling out*) Hi, Dad. It's me. I'm home.
Mr Chang	(*Off-stage*) Who's there?
Lina	It's me. Lina.
Mr Chang	I can hear you moving. I know you're there.

Lina sighs.

Lina (*Louder*) It's only me. Lina! (*To herself*) You can come out from under the bed now, Dad.

*Slowly, peering round the door, Mr Chang comes in from a bedroom off stage. Although it is late afternoon, he is wearing pyjamas. He looks **dishevelled**. It is clear he has been lying in the dust somewhere – Lina is probably right that he has been hiding under the bed since Mrs Chang went to work. At the same moment he steps into the living room, the elephant materialises from behind the sofa. Lina and Mr Chang pay no attention to it.*

Lina (*Holds out her hand in reassurance.*) See? There's no one else here, Dad. Only me.

Elephant	(*Direct to the audience.*) Well, I like that! That takes the biscuit that does! I do all I can to bring doom and gloom and misery to this place and Miss Short-Socks there pretends I'm not even here.
Mr Chang	You're late. Mum had to go to work. You know what time her shift starts, you should have been home.
Lina	Yes, I know, Dad. I'm sorry.
Mr Chang	But Lina, what if someone had come to the door and I'd been here on my own?
Elephant	HOW MANY TIMES? You are not alone, my friend! Never! I'm always here. Worrying you! **Tormenting** you! (*He circles round Mr Chang.*) And distressing you, of course. That's my favourite!
Lina	I said I'm sorry, Dad.
Elephant	Depression, **anguish**, anxiety, **melancholy**...I'm the fellow for the job.
Mr Chang	Where were you, Lina?
Elephant	Despondency? Discomfort? Worry? Let's save time, perhaps I should just get out my full Menu of Misery. (*He looks directly at the audience again.*) Any of you feel sad? Anxious? I can find you something if you like. A little panic perhaps, like Mr Chang here?
Lina	I just went out with a friend. She wanted to get some earrings. It was stupid...there's this thing on Saturday night.
Mr Chang	(*Sounding worried.*) Thing? What thing? Is it something I'm supposed to go to?
Elephant	Him go somewhere? That's funny. He's so depressed he hasn't stepped outside this flat for six years!
Lina	(*Shakes her head.*) No, Dad, you don't have to go. It's just a birthday party for Tanya, a girl in my class.
Mr Chang	Tanya? I don't think I've met her.

Lina	(*As if she is thinking about this.*) No, I don't think you have.
Elephant	Of course he hasn't! He never meets anyone! I've seen to that. Strangers – even school kids – are far too frightening for him.
Mr Chang	She'll have fun, I expect.
Lina	(*Sighs.*) Yeah. There's going to be a disco and a karaoke machine, I think. All the girls in my class are going.
Elephant	All except you, Cinders. You shan't go to the ball! (*He turns to the audience and pretends to look sad.*) No fairy tale ending here, I'm afraid. She has to stay and look after her poor old, sad dad who can't be left on his own! I tell you something, this girl could do with a pumpkin! Pity I don't have a magic wand! (*He laughs again, with no sympathy.*)
Mr Chang	I don't think you'll be able to go. Mum's working all weekend, Lina. (*He starts pacing up and down, quite agitated by the prospect.*) It's just not a good time. I just don't think you should go, Lina. I can't be on my own at the moment.
Lina	I know, Dad. It doesn't matter. It would have been fun but...
Elephant	But what? (*He puts his arms behind his head and lies down on the sofa as if he's sunbathing.*) Now there'll be a long awkward silence. I love those! (*He sighs contentedly.*) Beautiful! My work here is done!

Sure enough, Lina and Mr Chang say nothing. Lina rummages in her backpack. She is biting her lip a bit as if she might cry. But the tears won't actually come. She would have loved to go to the party, but it is not the first or the last time that she will be disappointed. She has got used to the fact that her father is ill and her free time cannot be the same as other children. She has to look after him – more as if she is the parent and he is the child. Her life is shaped by his depression.

Mr Chang goes to the window and stares out at the sea.

Elephant   It's me they won't talk about, you know! The elephant in the room! You can think of me as a dark cloud, if you like. But I think elephant is better — I'm big and heavy and grey. I'm Mr Chang's illness — his deep depression.

Mr Chang   (*Yawns.*) I'm tired.

Lina clears her throat but does not say anything.

Elephant   I touch everything this family does. (*He chuckles to himself.*) Or everything this family doesn't do, to be precise. Mr Chang gets panic attacks, you see. He can't bring himself to go outside. So, mostly, they don't do much at all, except sit around in the flat. It makes the whole family a bit sad, really. It's like there's one BIG elephant for Mr Chang (*he grins and flexes his muscles*) — that's me — but Mrs Chang and Lina sometimes have baby elephants — grim, cheerless low points — all of their own. They worry about Mr Chang. Sometimes that makes them sad…and, sometimes, furious. (*He nods towards Lina.*) Look at her now!

Lina thumps her school books down on the table.

Elephant	She won't say anything, though. I bet you she just shrugs her shoulders and offers him a cup of tea. You watch. Five, four, three, two, one...
Lina	(*Shrugs.*) How about a cup of tea, Dad?
Elephant	So predictable!
Mr Chang	That would be nice, love.
Lina	I'll get you a glass of water too. You can take your medication.
Elephant	(*Shifts uneasily.*) Oh no! Not the medication. That makes me sleepy. (*He hunches into a ball.*) It makes me shrink a bit, too!
Mr Chang	(*Still looking out at the sea.*) It's choppy out there today. But I can see a couple of boats.
Elephant	Here we go! Now he'll promise to take her out on a fishing trip...

Lina comes over with a tray. On it is a Chinese teapot, a glass of water and bottle of pills.

Lina	Take your tablets, then I'll make you some supper. Shall we have eggs?
Mr Chang	(*Swallowing his pills.*) If you like. I'm not very hungry.
Lina	How about scrambled? You like those. When we've eaten, I'll start on my science project, I think.
Mr Chang	I'm sorry about the party, Lina. I know you wanted to go.
Lina	It doesn't matter, Dad. I'm probably too busy anyway. My project is on earthworms...
Elephant	Now that is funny!
Lina	And there's loads of stuff to do for it. (*She laughs sadly to herself.*) I'm going to draw lots of pictures and graphs and things and colour them all in.
Mr Chang	Good girl. I tell you what... because you work so hard, we'll have a treat. As soon as I'm better, we'll hire a boat and I'll take you out on a fishing trip.
Elephant	And here we go... right on cue.
Mr Chang	We'll sail out to the Isle of Wight. Maybe we'll stay there for a couple of nights and then come back.
Lina	(*Tries to summon some enthusiasm. She has probably heard this a hundred times before but wants to believe it will come true.*) That would be brilliant, Dad.
Elephant	(*Closes his eyes.*) This makes me so weary!
Mr Chang	(*Really animated*) And we'll bring back the fish we catch and make a Chinese feast.
Elephant	...fatigued, debilitated and just plain knocked out!

(*He slumps back on the sofa and closes his eyes.*)

Mr Chang	When I was a little boy in China, I used to watch the fishermen out on their bamboo rafts.
Lina	With cormorants?

Elephant And now nostalgia. I've had enough. Good night. (*He begins to snore quietly.*)

Mr Chang Yes, of course, with cormorants. (*As he speaks the actor's voice begins to trail away and the scene ends, but we should be left with the impression that Mr Chang is enjoying his topic and talks for some time.*) The fishermen **domesticate** the birds, you see. A trained cormorant is a valuable asset. They catch the small fish until their throats are full and then they return to the raft or riverbank. The fishermen reward the birds and so it goes on. I remember once, I saw a cormorant catch over a hundred fish. Can you believe that, Lina? A hundred fish! One day, I'll take you to China and we'll see for ourselves. But first our fishing trip. We'll need to...

Scene 3

It is Monday morning. Lina and Caitlin are waiting for the bus to school. Caitlin has been talking for ages, telling Lina all the things she has missed out on at the weekend.

Caitlin ...and Tanya had this *HUGE* chocolate birthday cake. It was shaped like a microphone and they'd hired this proper singer – like a professional – to sing Happy Birthday.

Lina	Sounds lovely.
Caitlin	You *REALLY* should have been there. The best bit was the karaoke. Me and Bella sang this song together. We were SO bad. It was *REALLY* funny. But, actually, Tanya's brother said I had quite a good voice.
Lina	Oh...
Caitlin	Anyway, what did you do? Your science project?
Lina	(*Nods her head and looks down at her shoes but, suddenly, seems to have a change of heart.*) No. Actually, I was really busy this weekend. My dad hired a boat and took me on a fishing trip. We sailed out to the Isle of Wight and stayed in a really smart hotel. There was this band playing in the evening and they were FANTASTIC! Then, on the way home, these cormorants followed our boat, like they do in China. (*She mutters to herself.*) Well, almost like that anyway...

memoraid

Make Memory Lapses a Thing to Forget!

It may be tiny in size, but this astonishing new device developed in Switzerland could be about to dramatically raise standards in schools and universities across the world.

Using the latest MORF technology, the Memoraid is a device which fits snugly over the ear, and is connected electronically to a wireless transmitter that can be placed by the bedside when sleeping. This amazing device can then be digitally pre-programmed to identify and isolate particular areas of knowledge, for example history facts, or times tables. Memoraid then "fast tracks" relevant messages to the front of the memory queue, making them up to 98% more likely to be retained the next day.

People all over the world are already benefiting from the wonder of Memoraid:

Memoraid is totally awesome. I use it every week before my Math test and haven't got a question wrong for five months. I'm now the top achiever in 6th Grade.

I used Memoraid for three nights before my final Brain Surgery exams. The results were amazing. My brain feels like it's doubled in size! Now I can't imagine life without Memoraid.

Elly-May, in California

Manuel, in Madrid

But why take their word for it? Instant and total recall could be yours too!

Memoraid is manufactured in the UK by Swindles of Coventry. Contact them now for purchase details.

DON'T GET LEFT BEHIND, GET memoraid

I Believe in Unicorns

Michael Morpurgo

My name is Tomas Porec. I was seven years old when I first met the unicorn lady. I believed in unicorns then. I am nearly twenty now and because of her I still believe in unicorns.

My little town, hidden deep in its own valley, was an ordinary place, pretty enough, but ordinary. I know that now. But when I was seven it was a place of magic and wonder to me. It was my place, my home. I knew every cobbled alleyway, every lamp post in every street. I fished in the stream below the church, tobogganed the slopes in winter, swam in the lake in the summer. On Sundays my mother and father would take me on walks or on picnics, and I'd roll down the hills, over and over, and end up lying there on my back, giddy with joy, the world **spinning** above me.

I never did like school though. It wasn't the school's fault, nor the teachers'. I just wanted to be outside all the time. I longed always to be running free up in the hills. As soon as school was over, it was back home for some bread and honey – my father kept his own bees on the hillside – then off out to play. But one afternoon my mother had other ideas. She had to do some shopping in town, she said, and wanted me to go with her.

"I hate shopping," I told her.

"I know that, dear," she said. "That's why I'm taking you to the library. It'll be interesting. Something different. You can listen to stories for an hour or so. It'll be good for you. There's a new librarian lady and she tells stories after school to any children who want to listen. Everyone says she's brilliant."

"But I don't want to listen," I protested.

My mother simply ignored all my pleas, took me firmly by the hand and led me to the town square. She walked me up the steps into the library. "Be good," she said, and she was gone.

I could see there was an excited huddle of children gathered in one corner. Some of them were from my school, but they all looked a lot younger than me. Some of them were infants! I certainly did not want to be with them. I was just about to turn and walk away in disgust when I noticed they were all **jostling** each other, as if they were desperate to get a better look at something. Since I couldn't see what it was, I went a little closer.

Suddenly they were all sitting down and hushed, and there in the corner I saw a unicorn. He was lying absolutely still, his feet tucked neatly under him. I could see now that he was made of carved wood and painted white, but he was so lifelike that if he'd got up and trotted off I wouldn't have been at all surprised.

Beside the unicorn and just as motionless, just as neat, stood a lady with a smiling face, a bright flowery scarf around her shoulders. When her eyes found mine, her smile beckoned me to join them. Moments later I found myself sitting on the floor with the others, watching and waiting. When she sat down slowly on the unicorn and folded her hands in her lap I could feel expectation all around me.

"The unicorn story!" cried a little girl. "Tell us the unicorn story. Please."

She talked so softly that I had to lean forward to hear her. But I wanted to hear her, everyone did, because every word she spoke was meant and felt, and sounded true. The story was about how the last two magic unicorns alive on Earth had arrived just too late to get on Noah's ark with all the other animals. So they were left stranded on a mountain top in the driving rain, watching the ark sail away over the great flood into the distance. The waters rose and rose around them until their hooves were covered, then their legs, then their backs, and so they had to swim. They swam and they swam, for hours, for days, for weeks, for years. They swam for so long, they swam so far, that in the end they turned into whales. This way they could swim easily. This way they could dive down to the bottom of the sea. But they never lost their magical powers and they still kept

their wonderful horns, which is why there are to this day whales with unicorn's horns. They're called narwhals. And sometimes, when they've had enough of the sea and want to see children again, they swim up onto the beaches and find their legs and become unicorns again, magical unicorns.

After she had finished no one spoke. It was as if we were all waking up from some dream we didn't want to leave.

There were more stories, and poems too. Some she read from books, some she made up herself or knew by heart.

Then a hand went up. It was a small boy from my school, Milos with the sticky-up hair. "Can I tell a story, miss?" he asked. So sitting on the unicorn he told us his story. One after another after that they wanted their turn on the magical unicorn. I **longed** to have a go myself, but I didn't dare. I was frightened of making a fool of myself, I think.

The hour flew by.

"What was it like?" my mother asked me on the way home.

"All right, I suppose," I told her. But at school the next day I told all my friends what it was really like, all about the unicorn lady – everyone called her that – and her amazing stories and the fantastic magical storytelling power of the unicorn.

They came along with me to the library that afternoon. Day after day as word spread, the little group in the corner grew until there was a whole crowd of us. We would rush to the library now to get there first, to find a place close to the unicorn, close to the unicorn lady. Every story she told us held us **entranced**.

She never told us to sit still. She didn't have to. Each day I wanted so much to sit on the unicorn and tell a story, but still I could never quite summon up the courage.

One afternoon the unicorn lady took out from her bag a rather old and damaged-looking book, all charred at the edges. It was, she told us, her very own copy of *The Little Match Girl* by Hans Christian Andersen. I was sitting that day very close to the unicorn lady's feet, looking up at the book. "Why's it been burnt?" I asked her.

"This is the most precious book I have, Tomas," she said. "I'll tell you why. When I was very little I lived in another country. There were wicked people in my town who were frightened of the magic of stories and of the power of books, because stories make you think and dream; books make you want to ask questions. And they didn't want that. I was there with my father watching them burn a great pile of books, when suddenly my father ran forward and **plucked** a book out of the fire. The soldiers beat him with sticks, but he held on to the book and wouldn't let go of it. It was this book. It's my favourite book in all the world. Tomas, would you like to come and sit on the unicorn and read it to us?"

I had never been any good at reading out loud. I would always stutter over my consonants, worry over long words. But now, sitting on the magic unicorn, I heard my voice strong and loud. It was like singing a song. The words **danced** on the air and everyone listened. That same day I took home my first book from the library, *Aesop's Fables*, because the unicorn lady had read them to us and I'd loved them. I read them aloud to my mother that night, the first time I'd ever read to her, and I could see she was amazed. I loved amazing my mother.

Then one summer morning, early, war came to our valley and shattered our lives. Before that morning I knew little of war. I knew some of the men had gone to fight, but I wasn't sure what for. I had seen on television tanks shooting at houses and soldiers with guns running through the trees, but my mother always told me it was far away and I wasn't to worry.

I remember the moment. I was outside. My mother had sent me out to open up the hens and feed them, when I looked up and saw a single plane come flying in low over the town. I watched as it circled once and came again. That was when the bombs began to fall, far away at first, then closer, closer. We were all running then, running up into the woods. I was too frightened to cry. My father cried. I'd never seen him cry before, but it was from anger as much as fear.

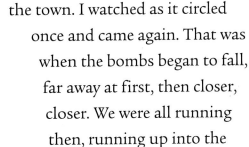

Hidden high in the woods we could see the tanks and the soldiers all over the town, **blasting and shooting** as they went. A few hours later, after they had gone, we could hardly see the town any more for the smoke. We waited until we were quite sure they had all gone, and then we ran back home. We were luckier than many. Our house had not been damaged. It was soon obvious that the centre of town had been hardest hit. Everyone seemed to be making their way there. I ran on ahead hoping and praying that the library had not been bombed, that the unicorn lady and the unicorn were safe.

As I came into the square I saw smoke rising from the roof of the library and flames licking out of the upper windows. We all saw the unicorn lady at the same moment. She was coming out of the library carrying the unicorn, **staggering** under its weight. I ran up the steps to help her. She smiled me her thanks as I took my share of the weight. Her eyes were red from the smoke. Between us we set the unicorn down at the foot of the steps, and she sat down exhausted, racked with a fit of coughing. My mother fetched her a glass of water. It must have helped because the coughing stopped, and all at once she was up on her feet, leaning on my shoulder for support.

"The books," she breathed. "The books."

When she began to walk back up the steps I followed her without thinking.

"No, Tomas," she said. "You stay here and look after the unicorn." Then she was running up the steps into the library, only to reappear moments later, her arms piled high with books. That was the moment the rescue began. People seemed suddenly to surge past me up the steps, and into the library, my mother and father amongst them.

It wasn't long before a whole system was set up. We children made two chains across the square from the library to the café opposite, and the books everyone rescued went from hand to hand, ending up in stacks on the floor of the café. The fire was burning ever more fiercely, the flames crackling, smoke billowing now from the roof. No fire engines came – we found out later the fire station had been hit. Still the books came out. Still the fire burned and more and more people came to help, until the café was filled with books and we had to use the grocer's shop next door.

The moment came when there were suddenly no more books to pass along and we all wondered why. Then we saw everyone coming out of the library, and last of all the unicorn lady, helped by my father. They came slowly down the steps together, their faces **smudged and blackened**. The unicorn lady sat down heavily on the unicorn and looked up at the burning building. We children all gathered around her as if waiting for a story.

"We did it, children," she said. "We saved all we could, didn't we? I'm sitting on the unicorn so any story I tell is true because we believe it can be true. We shall build our library up again just as it was. Meanwhile we shall look after the books. Every family can take home all the books they can manage and care for them. And when in one year or two or three we have our new library, then we shall all bring back our books, and we shall carry the magic unicorn inside and we shall all tell our stories again. All we have to do is make this story come true."

So it happened, just as the unicorn lady said it would. Like so many families in the town we took home a wheelbarrow full of books and looked after them. Sure enough the library was rebuilt just the same as the old one, only by now everyone called it the Unicorn, and we all brought our books back just as the unicorn lady had told it in her story.

The day the library opened, because I had helped carry the unicorn out, I got to carry him back up the steps with the unicorn lady, and the whole town was there cheering and clapping, the flags flying, the band playing. It was the proudest and happiest day of my life.

Now, all these years later, we have peace in our valley. The unicorn lady is still the town librarian, still reading her stories to the children after school. As for me, I'm a writer now, a **weaver of tales**. And if from time to time I lose the thread of my story, all I have to do is go and sit on the magic unicorn and my story flows again. So believe me, I believe in unicorns. I believe in them absolutely.

How Does a Story Become a Manga Graphic Novel?

Most novels rely almost entirely on words to tell the story, and use illustrations only to enliven the appearance of the book. A graphic novel, on the other hand, is a carefully-crafted balance of artwork and text. *Graphic* actually comes from the Greek word for "writing", but nowadays is used to describe diagrams and pictures, too.

Of all the different types of graphic novels, Japanese Manga could well be described as reaching the widest audience because it appeals to adults as well as children. Recently, Manga has become very popular in the UK.

So how does the process work? In order to translate a story into a Manga graphic novel the Manga artist has to decide which parts of the story are best shown in pictures, and which are best told in speech.

THE TREASURE OF SKULL ISLAND

Turn the page to find out more about how this graphic novel was made!

Take the following extract from *The Treasure of Skull Island*:

Captain Scarlet clamped his hand over the cook's mouth. "Hush, Slim! Stop! I think I heard someone," he whispered.

The sailors stood stock-still and listened. Captain Scarlet's face was a picture of concentration: every sinew was taut and his bushy eyebrows were creased in deep furrows. They could hear drips of water falling from the ceiling of the cave. They could hear the waves sloshing about around the entrance. Then, faint but distinct from the watery sounds of the cave, they heard a gentle hum of talk.

"Put out that torch!" ordered the Captain, still in a whisper. Slim grunted in agreement and the cave was thrown into darkness.

"Captain?"

"What, man?"

"I think we're trapped!"

The voices were getting louder and nearer. With a sinking fear, Captain Scarlet realised that he knew them. They belonged to the dreaded Black Beard and his cut-throat gang!

It could receive the Manga treatment in this way:

The action takes place in a cave, so in the book there's a passage to describe the cave setting. This isn't needed in a graphic novel. We can leave the description to the artwork and a short caption:

The speaker's volume and tone, and the urgency of the words, can be indicated by changing the outline of the speech bubble, increasing the font size or adding punctuation.

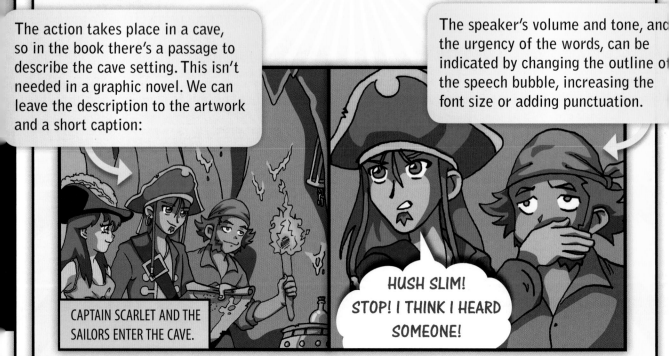

CAPTAIN SCARLET AND THE SAILORS ENTER THE CAVE.

HUSH SLIM! STOP! I THINK I HEARD SOMEONE!